I'm The Train Driver

Train drivers have a very important job.
They transport people and goods from place to place.
Now it's your turn to be the train driver!

illustrated by **David Semple**

OXFORD
UNIVERSITY PRESS

Great Clarendon Street, Oxford OX2 6DP
Oxford University Press is a department of the University of Oxford.
It furthers the University's objective of excellence in research, scholarship,
and education by publishing worldwide. Oxford is a registered trade mark
of Oxford University Press in the UK and in certain other countries

Text copyright © Oxford University Press 2022
Illustrations © David Semple 2022
Text written by Katie Woolley

British Library Cataloguing in Publication Data

Data available
ISBN: 978-0-19-278081-2

1 3 5 7 9 10 8 6 4 2

Printed in China

Paper used in the production of this book is a natural,
recyclable product made from wood grown in sustainable
forests. The manufacturing process conforms to the
environmentalbregulations of the country of origin.

My name is

_____

and today I'm the train driver!

Today your job is to drive the train from the railway depot to its final destination.

This family are going sightseeing in the city.

First you need to put on your uniform.
What do you need to wear to be a train driver?

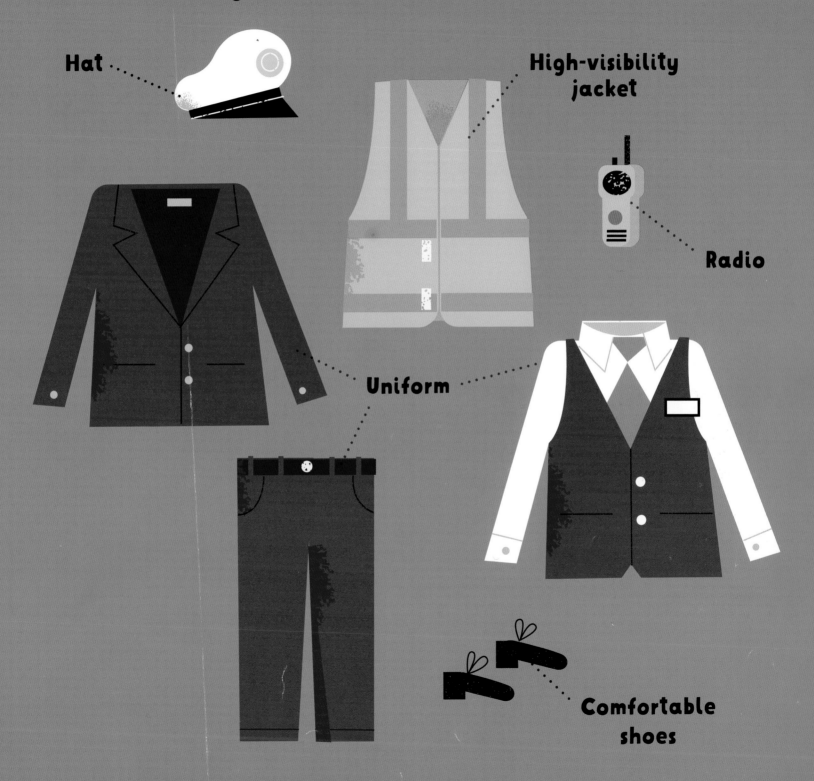

Hat

High-visibility jacket

Radio

Uniform

Comfortable shoes

This is your train!
Can you name all the parts?

Carriage

Roof

Door release button to open passenger door

Buffer that protects the train and absorbs jolts

Wheel

Let's count how many carriages there are!
1, 2, 3. Well done! What colour are they?

Window

Driver's cab

Engine

Gangway that joins carriages together

Door

Coupler that joins two trains together

It's time to climb into your cab.
Put on your seatbelt and check your controls.

START/STOP
engine button

Emergency
stop

Radio

Throttle

Horn

When you're ready, twist the green button to start the engine. Then push the black throttle lever to move the train forwards.

CHOO, CHOO!
You're off!

Track

Brake

Speed dial

Door button

Headlights

Your first station stop is up ahead.
How many passengers can you see on the platform?

Station

Conductor

Read your speed dial to check your speed. Pull the red brake lever backwards to stop the train.

Signal

Platform

When you have stopped, press the purple button to open the doors.

Your passengers are on board and the signal has turned green. It's safe for you to head off down the track!

TOOT, TOOT!

Push the throttle to pick up speed again.
Don't forget to toot your horn and wave hello
to the people on the bridge!

A freight train is travelling on the tracks today, too.
This freight train is carrying building materials.
What objects can you see? What shapes are they?

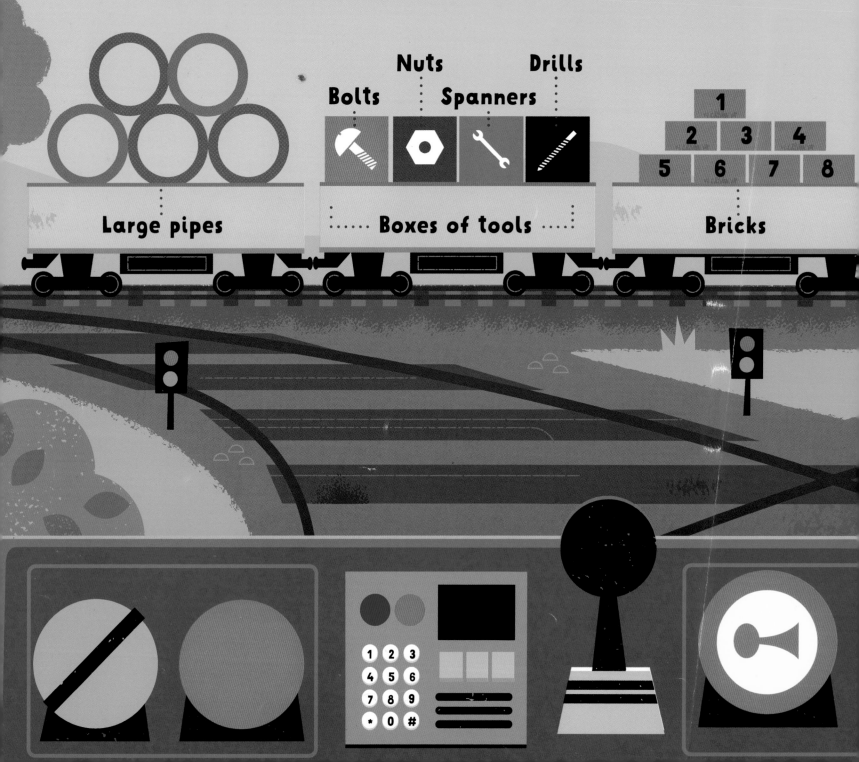

Bolts

Nuts

Spanners

Drills

1

2 3 4

5 6 7 8

Large pipes

Boxes of tools

Bricks

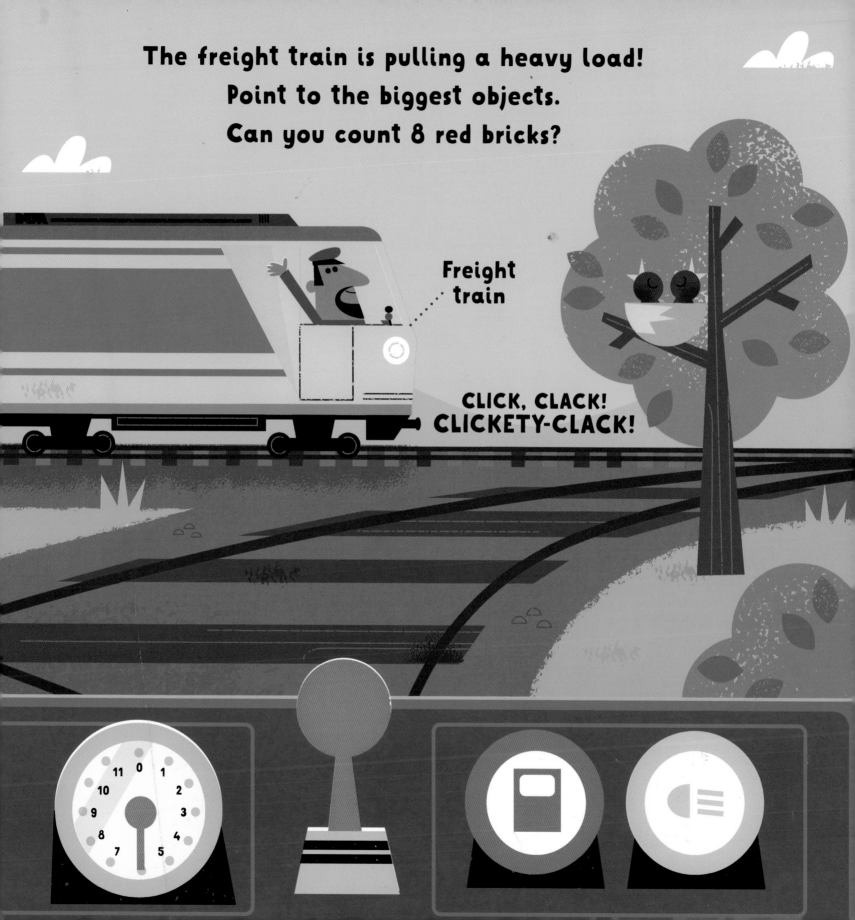

The freight train is pulling a heavy load!
Point to the biggest objects.
Can you count 8 red bricks?

Freight
train

CLICK, CLACK!
CLICKETY-CLACK!

Watch out, there's a tunnel ahead!
The train needs to travel slowly through it.

Check your speed. Pull on your brake and count
backwards as you slow down – 5, 4, 3, 2, 1.

Top
speed
6

Then press the yellow button to turn on your headlights. It will be dark inside the tunnel!

Don't forget to beep your horn as you head into the pitch black. **TOOT, TOOT!**

On the other side of the tunnel is a level crossing.
Turn your headlights off. Push your throttle to
pick up a bit of speed now, too. The vehicles have
stopped to let your train pass safely by.

Van

Van

Bike

Car

Van

Look at the order pattern of the vehicles.
What vehicle will join the back of the queue next?

Bike

Car

Barrier

You need to switch tracks. Is it left or right to the city? Look at the signs and follow the arrow. Then push the throttle to pick up speed. Your passengers have somewhere to be!

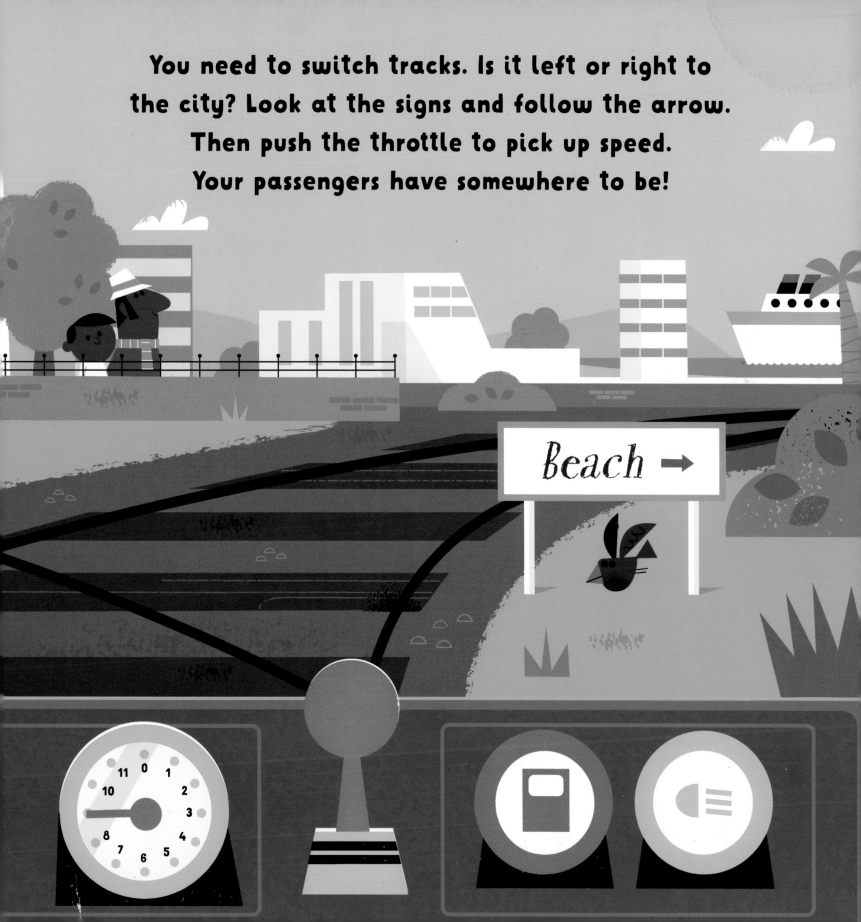

Beach →

Hurray! You've reached the city's main station and have come to a stop. Your passengers have got off and are on their way.

Twist the green button to switch off the engine.
Then wave goodbye to your passengers.

Well
done!

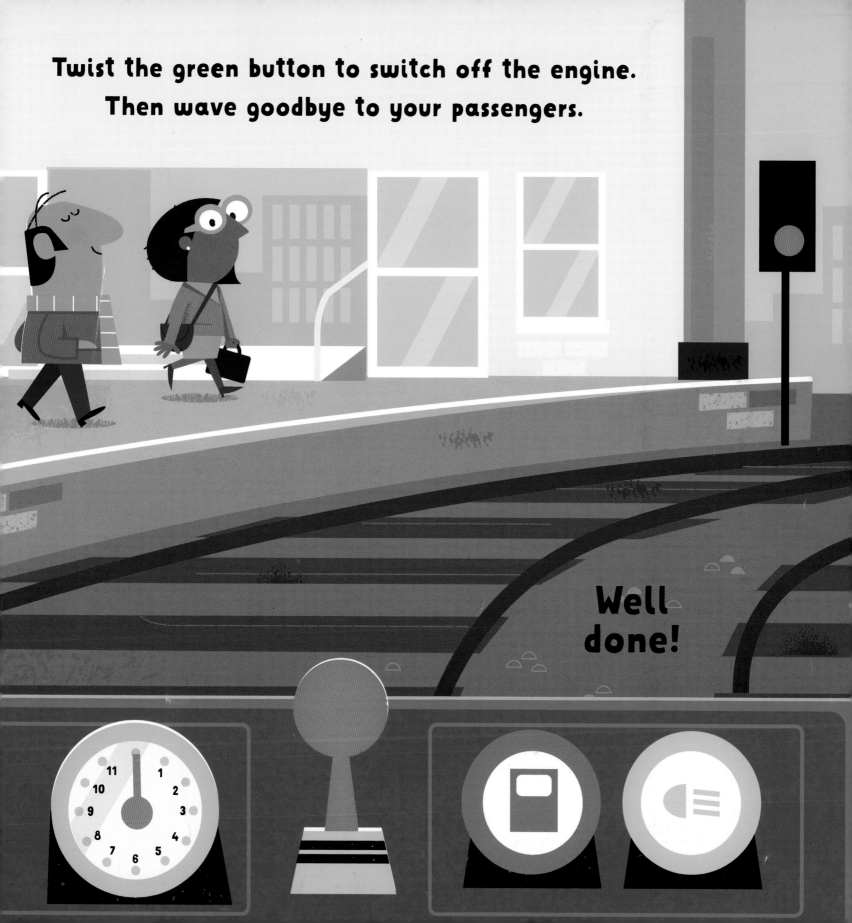

There's just one job left to do.
Log your arrival time with the control room.
Which driver number are you?

It's time for a rest before you head back home!

Goodbye!

Driver number 6